Troubled Tongues

Poetry by Crystal Williams:

Kin
Lunatic

3.8.09

For Sharon + Sin
Beauty, Blessings
to you +
your family.

TROUBLED
TONGUES

Poems by

Crystal Williams

Lotus Press
Detroit

First Edition

International Standard Book Number: 978-0-9797509-1-5
Library of Congress Control Number: 2008942336

Printed and manufactured in the United States of America

Lotus Press, Inc.
"Flower of a New Nile"
Post Office Box 21607
Detroit, Michigan 48221
www.lotuspress.org

Acknowledgments

My gratitude to the editors of the following
journals and anthologies where some of these
poems first appeared: *The American Poetry
Review, 5AM, Cream City Review, Luna, Fourth
River, Court Green, The Indiana Review,
Columbia Poetry Review, The Electronic Poetry
Review, The Oregonian, Efforts and Affections,
Rainbow Darkness,* and *Thirtysomething American
Thirtysomething Poets.*

Terrance Hayes, A. Van Jordan, and Amanda
Moore were very helpful during the early stages
of this book's making. I'd especially like to thank
Yona Harvey and Lisa Steinman for their close
reading, insightful comments and patience. I
couldn't imagine being guided and cheered on by
better poets or people. To my other friends and
family: I bow.

Finally, portions of this book were generously
supported by The Levine Fund. Thank you.

For Uncle

Contents

III.

"How astonishing it is that language can almost mean,
and frightening that it does not quite. Love, we say,
God, we say, Rome and Michiko, we write, and the words
get it all wrong."

(from "The Forgotten Dialect of the Heart," by Jack Gilbert)

Invocation

Let me mash my tongues.
Let the lost language
& red pulp of them be laid to earth
then to the earth water.
Let grow from this a white
blossoming tree. Let bloom
a shade broad & deep
as my dead mother's shadow
which rests on the plate before me
alongside what more I need:
a modest pear, a spike of wheat,
a loaf of bread.

I

Rituals

Old, this ritual, hand cradling foot.
Here, in Vogue Nails, hunched & humble
they wash, scrub, polish our feet.
When Beauty walks in we all look up
& ogle—entranced. She is exquisite,
a mix of men, dark & light, maybe Persian
or some domestic blend. It doesn't matter
to the young girl in the middle chair
who this morning tried her very best:
her whitest bustier, her dear pink scalloped skirt.
& for a moment she was lovely.
But here, now, her face is full-on torrent:
astonishment, bewilderment, & then anger
settle into a sour glower. Always swift,
this moment of death & birth:
the young girl oblivious to the world,
the young woman beginning to grasp its edges.
I am saddened that this regular girl
now knows she is regular, understands
something of what will never be.

I want to go over & say something,
but it is a private moment
& there is nothing here but loss:
the husky quiet of the forest trees,
the moment the world rustles unevenly
& you know nothing of it
& you understand nothing
but that you cannot change it.

5

Beauty [aloud]

Beauty moved into the building six months ago & suddenly all our shabbiness grew shabbier: The mailbox doors wouldn't shut, someone duct-taped the hall carpet after Lil Quan tripped & knocked his grown-tooth out, trash overflowed, & then Demetria held another one of her "protests" by withholding rent—even though her rent was already two months late. Beauty was loud, walked as if an elephant had taken up residence in her small, beautiful bones; & was rude: never did introduce herself properly. Plus, quiet as is kept, Beauty was obvious (& not *that* beautiful). She wore tight pants & weird wigs, some long & black & sleek as all of sleekdom, others blond, red, & purple plum. We girls clucked she was an actress or a whore, maybe both, before Mrs. Gilbert chided, "Children, that sho' ain't no working girl—she ain't never touched no work & ain't no work ever touched her." & right about then, Mr. Jenkins started showing up, hemmed & hawed about late rent, sucked his gapped teeth, stuck out his stomach more than it already was. But as far as we could see, Beauty didn't care what anyone said, stood her ground, nodding "yes," she thought people ought to pay rent, pay their way, "no," she didn't mean to take advantage, but, well, you see, things weren't going so well for her & didn't he understand. We regular folk gnawed on gossip. *Beauty is a broke-down bitch & is getting put out, & God don't like ugly, & ya get what you give!* But the men, poor devils, nearly lost their minds: took up arms, scurrying around the building like ants under attack, to this corner & that, throwing rent parties no women would go to, trying to dissuade Mr. Jenkins (when they ought to have been pleading to Mrs. Jenkins). The men, the men—those wayward believers—stealing beauty away as if all colonies require a queen from whom nothing is expected or earned. But without our help there was no way. So Beauty was evicted, got kicked to the curb. Now the men have gone about their business and woe, though the world has quieted its incessant accusations. & life is surely sweeter without Beauty stomping above my head.

Azalea

The cut flowers, how they thrive, my friends.
A million girls for a million hands.
Over & over they fill the vase, the pot,
the sweet house, the heart. But for Azalea
one needs a practical plot.
She is not, after all, the sad-eyed tulip,
the cocky aster, the orchid, the ingénue.
She regards the seasons in all their trouble & glee,
quietly watches her sisters hastily taken up.
I pray this once, this year, dear God,
let someone find sweet Azalea enough.

Polliwog

No one should be this beautiful,
I think. *She's fucking it up for the rest of us.*
I'd forgotten how in light of such extravagance
men's heads purl in unison, eyes quickening,
feet suddenly sucked to their impossible
floor & how women's hands don't bother to smooth
their hair, but stay clasped, lips agape, eyes hesitating
then casting fearfully aside. There is that kind of beauty
& I swim midst it today, watch it gleam & glide,
over fries, beer, remember God is real
& having fun with the lot of us.
We talk, she & I, about love, passion,
a man who is good but perhaps not good enough. For her,
always another. She has thought it out:
What would love be without passion? she sighs.
Between us grow such different questions. *Where*
is love? I ask, imagining it in the deeps—
below the water's raging, where it is calm,
patient. Under this, I watch her beautiful
blink & smile, poke a fry, swig beer, translucent
& sad, shimmering at top.

The Men

sit on the stoop
just inside the spot of sun
& chatter over this & that,
professorial banter,
their shoulders hunched
as small boys hunch,
sticks in hand, stooping
at water's edge, giggling.
When the young girl canters by
they stop. All silence
& possibility. They dare not mutter
& it may not be in them to say & so:
heavy, the wind, its silence,
their eyes. Her breasts
sway, her small skirt flips the wind
back its playful taunt.
& the three still
as well water
well after she has gone.
Their lives suddenly smaller,
the water's edge nothing
to be giggled at, deep & cobalt
& hopelessly resolved.

Wake

~for Yo & T, U & A

& how she, the daughter, the niece,
among the other nieces & cousins
was one minute squealing, buoyant,
& in the next too much of us,
her body laden with the full sadness of the day
& how her father, mid sentence, whipped his head
around & whisked across the room towards her
& how in the exact moment
his arm scooped through the air her body
bowed to it & how they made for themselves
on the hill over there a perch, balm,
the two, father & daughter
& how lucent, the stark, brimming sky & how
the world slowed, though the children played,
& there was laughter even on this day,
& there were chicken & beans & cobbler,
cake & how the old women wiped the kitchen
& how people sprawled heavy
& how the mother, from deep in the room
suddenly made her way outside
as if someone had whispered
what no one could have whispered & how
the sweet boy, batman in hand, too
made his way from a different quadrant
& how they sat, the daughter, the father,
mother & son, words between them, yes,
but from here—silent,

on the grass, the sun so bright on their backs
as to make four bodies appear as one
undulating tumulus, pulsing black along the horizon
& how the sister, the aunt, for whom this day,
seemed to be gently moving everything about:
clearing the clouds, shifting bodies, divulging
what she knew of beauty & how.

Parable of Divas
Aretha Franklin & Diana Ross

Back in the day, Ree Ree & Miss D were sweet meat, ours
to pick over like vultures. We were Detroiters; after all,
it was duty to learn from our lost.

ReeRee's house had an untended yard.
D was in flat-out denial: Detroit had given her nothing
&, be damned, she'd return the favor.

We sucked our teeth, harrumphed:
*They're trifling, look, see, fortune has knocked
& the hussies have gained amnesia.*

We were too young to know survival, song, is enough;
combined they are testimony in a city so Black. We thought,
no. Tend yard, offer back. Savor the sweet stuff of our city.

& yet we too moved, forgot the chance gardeners
& thankless hussies of youth, became them
in varying degrees, in spite of ourselves. Unavoidable, this.

There is always some pigeon nipping at the shoelace
because it is there & speaks to stature. Aretha & Diana's
contradictions should have readied me:

from respectable people, damning affronts.
From damnable people, beauty. I cannot be fully convinced
of any good thing. There is no such thing

13

as a measure for loss. There is only Ree Ree & Miss D trilling:
Silly girl, nothing is so sweet
as not to be sour, somehow, some way.

Girls in Tornado

It smelled bad, she tells the interviewer, like everything
in the world all at once, the tornado pulling up the earth
& its secrets. It is not the wind that kills you

but everything picked up along the way. The wind's machine
gun propels rocks & wood, chunks of houses, cars, bodies,
travesties. There is no hiding from them.

She believes it was angels she heard wailing, screaming
for backup to help prop the walls up around the scared,
cowering people. She insists they were fighting it out

with the demons who were shoving the walls inward
from the other side. That the folk are alive is proof: good
prevails, she thinks.

I want to tell her it is never that simple

& wonder what will become of her belief.
Will it pick up debris along the way or will it remain simple?
Can her walls withstand the struggle between sides,

or will she get crushed among other sufferers? I wonder

what became of that young girl & in what manner she'll learn
that just as during a tornado you should be fearful
when there is nothing, no movement, no startling,

so too should you fear a woman on edge, a woman whose eyes
no longer assert the angels or their brother demons.
A woman, a friend, who is tearless & silent, decided & ready
to dig down into the earth & pull up everything,
pull up everything all at once.

~ *after Reetika*

Night Bloom

~ for Jade, after Hayden

It makes no sense to say *things will get better*
because you will not understand until they *are* better
& they may not get better soon. There is always pain
in the world & you have seen so much of it.
I do not know how to explain other than to say,
I am so sorry your mother has died, Girl,
that her mother has turned her back, that your father
is a rogue & you are having to do this grown-up work alone.
I would like to tell you to be patient
but understand that right now you might only know fear.
Listen, then. & know this: it is okay to be fearful.
If you cannot believe that things will soften,
trust that I believe for you.
You will not remember all of this pain.
But when Darkness insists you attend his party
you will know the trapdoors & gloomy corners of that house.
& you alone will be able to find the garden
where beautiful Cereus is opening her eyes in the pitch black.

Your Father's Face

~ for Mel, after Eddie

It is slow, the forgetting of a face. This is how it goes:
the edges blur, flesh & blood pull away from their skull.
& one day, gone. You'll think yourself an awful daughter.
Surely a father's face should remain sharp as first light.
So like all of us who are without, you'll rummage
through the boxes of your mind, searching & finding nothing
but books, each holding another truth, a bigger,
more succulent lesson. But you won't want lessons. So
you'll continue to unpack
until nothing makes sense, until the stories of your life
whirl & clamor & whirl & whirl
& all the while your heart like all hearts will moan
& lament its circumstance.
But the heart is a beautiful monster,
it nearly always survives its fate. Believe me when I say
it is not a picture you seek. Someday
when you have given in to the lost images of your father
& your girl body relaxes finally into womanhood,
someone will ask a question
for which you should have no answer, but you will answer
& the soft tissue of your body for that second
will look leaner, more male & for a moment
gloriously beyond you.

Note to Niece About a Breakup

Outside the jewelry store with its gleam & bling bling,
a bee beats its wings against the window.
Inside: a series of fantastical flowers, silks & taffetas
bunched craftily & strung.
& although the window is unclean,
pitted with a month's worth of world-spew & debris,
the bee has seen; everything in her famished body
insists the fantasy, the cold, cruel ruse is true.
& so she whips her wings with persistence
she cannot well sustain. She is hopeless, furious
& flinging ever towards the idea of it.

The Horse

His name was Sunny. He was Arabian
& mine, mean & tempered, he'd stiffen up,
buck & snort, nip at my hands.

The body does not always reflect its heart.
When with you I mean to say, *Love,*
caress me, run your hand along my back.

Between two bodies is the world
& its circumstance, our hearts & old wounds,
sometimes enough to make Time
pack her bags & hobble away.
This weight is a saddle.
There is nothing more I can tell you
but that I rein myself in, even now;
nothing more to offer but a slow sigh,
a regret galloping into the long field.

Lace

~ after James

In the Boys & Girls Club
I stopped him mid-dart,
pointed to his shoes. "Boy,
you're gonna fall on your face."
He hesitated, then bent down,
each hand grabbing a lace
each lace its own world.
Right towards left, left under,
loop, loop, knot. Oh, how he toiled
to make them one.
      After a year I am sure
he has forgotten his own deliberate hands,
can close his eyes & from memory, habit,
tie the laces—considers the two strands
a single thing.
      Love. We forget.
Our hurts cannot always be bound
to our healings. In matters like this
we must slow, take note of what & how
we loop, of how & where we knot.

Parable of the Chicken Wing

~ after Robyn

I have hustled recipes as if they were lovers,
spread them flat, put my feet
& back into, spilled over them
all sorts of raw & red things; I have burned
pots & have scars enough as proof.
Here now, another pot luck,
each lugging a similar thing. Baby,
we been tongue & paw for days
& still I tire of the shallow pan.
My nights grow deep
& my shelves buckle, bulge,
moan their dismay. Truth of it is,
sweet tongue of a boy,
fire ain't always the same kinda hot
(& that means you ain't eating tonight
'cause my wings always seem to be done,
while baby, yours do not).

Lesson

~ after Freida

When the circus comes to town,
do not circle the tent & kneel at a hole
hoping to catch a peek.
When some roadie catches your penniless self
& asks if you want to go in, do not whisper,
I don't know. Know what you want,
she said, & tell everyone who will listen.

Playground: Ars Poetica

We run wild, play hide-n-seek
in the big park at the end of the block,
dip in & out of the jungle gym,
hang upside down when folks are looking,
showing off. We made up a secret language:
Bernard did _____ under the swing set
& John John & me know why.
LaMonica saw a lady & man _____
& ran & told her momma. So Biddy's D=
Bernard's dookie; the man & woman =
Getting Funky in the Cabbage Patch.
We got a world on our tongues!
We run & jump & skip & jive.
　　But Momma says
the world is bigger than our block,
& hanging from the jungle gym,
no matter how much panty you show,
becomes less clever by the day;
says we shouldn't be surprised
when other kids claim we're stuck up
& won't come around anymore & why should they
if we won't invite them to play?
So pretty much they leave us be
& here we are, playing hide-n-seek &
whispering our secret language
while every now & again
some gumpy newbie wanders over & shouts,
Hey, y'all! Come out, come out wherever you are.

Happiness [aloud]

Happiness was a little cockeyed & her dress was a peculiar yellow & when she laughed she sounded, well, something like to a donkey. But our boy Ollie was not a little bit thick. I mean, when he was younger he cried & yelped even when he'd hoarded all the Legos. & it wasn't that he was a stupid boy or even a blind boy. He was just, well, stubborn. So, it came to be on that bright Sunday afternoon, that Happiness & her cockeyed self & Ollie & his thick-headed self converged in a grand, full-blown, down & dirty misunderstanding. Birds cawed, dogs romped, folks milled around. At one point, some kid stuck his head under Happiness' dress until his momma yanked him out. See, Happiness, though cockeyed, had excellent hearing. "But I am here, you've been calling & I've come." & Ollie kept saying, "But you're cockeyed & I don't want cockeyed happiness." "Well," she huffed, "I'm what you've got!" Meanwhile, Patience, whose friends mostly called him Pat because his given name sounded feminine & he wasn't, went to the park to see what had kept his daughter away. He found her next to the teeter-totter in that odd yellow dress, staring down some fool of a boy who himself was no Adonis. Pat sat on the bench for an hour before finally pulling a crying Happiness away. After she'd gone, Ollie stood for some time feeling not quite right. Smaller children ran around him, a dog used his leg. & at 8:05 post meridian, our boy Ollie realized it was cold & dragged his sorry butt home. You know the rest. He ate, he shat & took some months to figure out that any Happiness is better than none.

Cosmology

& long after it had been done, the light & sky, the water
bridging the bodies, the long repeated & entwined histories,
their correspondent travesties, we were left with one boy

bopping pea-headed down the street, his gruff yellowing dog,
a suspicious series of familiar inhabitants lining the blocks
of our boy's house. To the west

The Old Guys, to the east, The Wives' Tales, directly north,
the Heart clan, & south—the Parables all warring & jiving
in need to be supreme, understood, the light. This locus,

nadir & pinnacle on Chicago's southern most chin,
these four small blocks, the greystones piled high & tight,
the iron sentinels lined up in a horizon of black atop black,

combined create so much confusion & beauty the trees waver
& sway, hold their palms to their foreheads as if to faint.
Who can make anything of it? Surely not the many voices

rumbling low & faint, echoing along Cottage Grove, MLK,
Ellis, St. Lawrence, all. The birds too echo, warn & call
along their perches. It is madness here. I tell you, madness.

Do you see the girls at the corner cackling? They screech
because who cares that the Old Guys mutter,
the Wives' Tales' high moral ground? What fool listens

29

to the Heart's unenviable moans? No. They cackle & gossip
about boys & boots, suck Now-N-Laters, drink juicy-juicy,
& paint their nails.

So, though things are blooming again & brave people are
returning to this once deserted corner, what of us once lost
has not yet, might never, return.

& among it: our burdens, sliding along the blocks, learn
& so disguised they hint to Ollie. Oh, they fiercely whisper
to Ollie. & if he listened, what would they say these Greek

gods renamed Demetria & Darnell in their golden
party boots, these morals with their night candles & capes
creeping on the block in the middle night, on the down low,

these apprehensions desperate & digging deeper as if miners;
is it they who sound like, *thump-thump, thump-thump*?
Here in this: the aggregate of our lives

& a boy bopping under the street's harsh lights,
bumping into the real & unreal, too young to understand
the tongue's troubled ways or its constant pitiful strain to say.

Girls on Porch

Dear Girls,

I moved away a year after I saw you on your porch,
am writing after a lovely Rosh Hashanah dinner.
How appropriate that in the moment of challah
& gefilte fish, when things begin anew
& people are to beg forgiveness
for the year's past grievances,
I was reminded of the solitary drive,
the manacle of my vehicle & its dividing
which that night seemed especially acute,
& you girls
on your blue porch, a perfect portrait:
rat tail comb in the hand of one,
the second sitting on a vinyl kitchen chair,
high backed, black glossy legs
connecting her to the ground,
her hair wild & pouting
as if demanding to be kept free,
while the third of you, hands on hips,
mouth open, jacked her jaw, tilted her head
& let out what I took to be a laugh,
a single gleaming bulb above your heads
as if an ancient star & light washed your dark bodies
with yellow. I thought: We are sisters beneath this glow,
even though even now I prove unable to feel
or sound fully of you. Every other truth was whisper
& shadow: Sam Cooke crying his heart raw

on a distant radio, some body cooking,
some other body playing cards in a basement,
some young boy bumping & grinding
against some young girl.   If this knowing is love,
how I loved you girls & ghosts. How I wanted
to stop my slick wheels, the foreign engine
dividing the path's dark glow, not just slow the roll,
drive-by eye, but get out, lay to my fissured tongue
the sweet candy of your language,
freeze the frame & draw myself faintly in.

Telegram

To Whom It May Concern,

The Old Guys have retired:
Poseidon insists he's a seal,
runs butt-naked
through the retirement home
flipping everyone off
with his one good "flipper";
Zeus' meds make him cranky &
Hades retired to Arizona,
works part-time at a Krispy Kreme. Stop.
Eurydice wears heavy-duty bras. Stop.
All have wisely avoided Florida
& want you to know they are fine.
Stop. Well adjusted & eating good.
Stop. They are sorry to have not written,
but understand they are
well remembered.
Stop. Do not send money:
Their 403k's are working out. Stop.

The Wives' Tales
Chicago, IL

All That Glitters Ain't Gold, eyes shiny as Easter morning,
had news from BoPeep's Bakery where
Crazy As a Road Lizard held up the store at 7:15 am,
just 15 minutes after it opened
& would have taken away $11.76 had he not been caught by
Oh No You Didn't who carted his ragged tail to jail.

God Is Good—who was in her red apron & red dress
(which meant she had a new sweetest
& was planning on cooking later in the day)
sucked her breath hard enough to make the earth shake,
got sad & thought, "Oh my, do I ever wish *Crazy*
was something more than a hot, crazy mess."

You Get What You Give twiddled his fingers,
snickering until *God Don't Like Ugly*
harrumphed & crossed her chunky arms
at which *Get* lowered his head & got quickly quiet.

Things Will Get Better broke their silence:
"I have," *Things* whispered, "a question."
A question! But, oh, oh!
What to do? They were ill-equipped
& a question could only set them all a'titter & askew.
"What will happen to *Crazy*? What will be done?"
After a moment's confusion, *Don't Cry* chirped:
"Well, whatever happens, one can't cry over,"

& all chimed, "Spilt milk!" so gleefully that
their particular corner of the earth quaked
dry its night's dew.

Satisfied that the question wouldn't be their demise,
around & around they went until,
bits of sagaciousness exhausted,
they could again stand as they most liked:
quiet, unthinking, content.

As the day's sun slunk,
the Tales bid one another adieu
leaving *Everything for a Reason*
grumbling on his stoop.

Everything had for years held vigil
over his boy, the boy's mother, uncle
& grandmother, & *Everything* wanted out.

He was tired of these people
to whom the Tales were intolerably adhered.
He grimaced at the thought of another day
when *Everything's* foolish child
with his dumb blank eyes
would pull the white cat's tail,
stomp a fat, dragging roach,
lift five coins from his mother's purse,
then go cause trouble at Deante's house.

& on the way back to the block the pea-headed boy
against the wisdom of the sun
or the loud-talking moon
would invert his directions, get befuddled,
a bit more than a bit confused,
stand on the corner of Oakwood & Cottage Grove
sniffling & misunderstanding,
as is the way of his folks,
the many simple & honest
languages surrounding them,
lost. Indeed, even among so much, lost.

Parable of Ancestors
New York, NY*

There was no poetry in the men who erected these buildings
atop the twenty thousand Africans nestled beneath
this ground, here in the middle of our great city.
There was no one to say, "Stop,
you, respect & let them rest."
Instead, the buildings grew up,
the city groaned & stretched itself wide & wide.
The millions of stories packed one on top of the other:
ghosts bumping & pulling around the city's great halls,
whispering around the neighborhoods until someone heard,
said, "Wait, our brothers' bones are under here.
Shouldn't we dig them up?"

If our world is to work & make good & true, make due,
leave them be where they are but write it in the books
that the children will read & be tested on.
Holding up this great American city, this great
America: the bones of our brothers. This is our closet,
children, bones & buildings & blood. No bigger truth
than this: In the dark crevices, over top & underneath
are the dark bones, the dark bloods. Everywhere.

---

*From 1712-1790, upwards of twenty thousand freed & enslaved Africans
were buried in a five- to six-acre site in New York City. The burial ground
was discovered in the 1990s.

Portrait of a Poet

~ for Major Jackson

Once, in the brownest city in the country
in the biggest high school in the brownest city
in the country was a girl among girls who
everyday bathed, dressed, ate grits, eggs
& took two city buses to school.
The girl among girls believed in many mysteries
not least of which was the word
as she had once heard it said,
The word is the only thing that can both
hold hostage & free/confine & define.
& this seemed true. For once, she had heard
her father curse & pray & her mother apologize.
So, everyday this brown girl in her brown city
went searching, knelt to the dusty stacks
of her school's library, gently pulling
the narrow volumes from their shelves,
laying her tender ear against their gloss,
hoping to hear someone else
clear & soundly call her name.
Let me say it again: Somewhere in this land
is a girl among girls whose belief is pure, unwavering
& holy. She holds her hopeful ear to the books.
Her ear is to the books, still
& searching.

Theon's #5 Nail Lacquer

All the hoes wore it,
  which made us preps
jones even more.

When attended properly,
  as if by providence
that boring matte burgundy

changed into the most
  luminescent, sparkling
red. & in that transformation

is all I have ever needed to know:
  what seems dull is dull
until you spit-shine it.

All you need is a good clear coat
  & you're good to go, baby,
glitter & gold.

Boxed, or
When *I* Consider the African American

~ for Terrance Hayes

I.

The poet pokes her pinpoint nose into the mix & although I did not solicit her opinions says, *I like your older, less discursive work.* I nod because it is the thing I have been trained to do. I know she means the black girl stories, black boys, beauty shops, beat boxing on some stoop, each blunt quarrel dipped in metaphor, translation, bedeviled tongue (this of mine), coated with places I should've been/have been/ should be, the metaphors she expects, does not know intimately but thinks she knows, wants to know for some reason all her own.

II.

Dear Reader,

this is a box in the box a
triangle in the triangle a
circle in the circle a
period in the period a
world, jury-rigged with
meaning,
but just one world. Still,
it is easy to do & so let
us *not* forget the box, its
shape & form, its lyric
implication,
discursive meaning
in opposition to
(in use of!)
other forms. Though,
true.
Abstracted it is a box.
In narrative it is a box.
Combined: two forms,
superimposed,
deepened
& deepening, something
more into which we
reach,
something more from
which we emerge.

41

♌

Oh, let us say it thus:
what is the use of color
if there is to be only one
sunrise, repeating its
shallow heart over &
over?

Oh, let us say it thus:
both quarrel & stem can
pierce a hard heart.

Oh, this is tautological,
repetitive & repeating.

III. T,

I know you see it, this, where I am, in the circle,
in the box, the period emphasizing some finality,
all the while: trying to make something of it
like some loopy cook, arms & digits mucked with flour.
So what if it is pasta w/pigs feet, cornmeal w/scallops?
Surely there must be room for the confluence
of languages (flavas!) in some place other than
my head. Isn't spanglish a thing? Isn't tuckus a butt?
Pass me the damned pie pan, man!

Let us say it thus: there are too many angles
& too few roundabouts. T, I'm at the Starbucks
wanting gingerbeer, at Safeway hoping for danger.
The unexpected is our last horizon & where else
are we to poke, to cook, to talk in our peculiar way?

You asked a question, although I am not sure
a question was your intention.

When *I* consider the African American I conflate
a lyric: think a budding branch covered with snow,
its slow, inevitable bow, the heavy aggregate sagging,
the swift snap back, to, upwards.

When I consider the African-American
I think of that poet, her choice of words,
where she would have me   & mine,

the locus from which she would take me,
what she would take from me.
I think of your daughter, the sweet, fat body
I held so many years ago,
how she evolves year by year
into something long, cylindrical,
her eyes wider than a child's eyes,
her fingers, longer than a child's fingers, as if
she is reaching for something not quite hers just yet,
as if she has already seen something
not quite hers just yet, & I pray;
think of her body as our body—
its vessel clean & clear
for now, its inhabitant
treasured & clean
for now, not bowed to the ground
by discourse or lyric
but erect on its own & shooting, shooting.

III

How to Become a Black Woman
(while being/having been raised by a white woman)

~ for Ross Gay

1. In fifth grade have Miss Kevera charge you with telling redheaded Marshall that his body odor has become a problem.

2. In sixth grade move to Madrid & when the girls at the Catholic private school ask, "Africana?" respond, "No! Americana."

3. Move back to America where you promptly get surrounded on the playground, accused of being saddity (read: trying to be white). Talk your way out of the beat down. Go home & practice clipping the sharp wings from your words, leaving only the rounded middle-bellies. Likewise, practice "shit," "fuck," "motherfucka," & "hell," over & over until their vexed edges are at the ready.

4. Keep secret from your peers & mother that you ply yet a third language.

5. Get through high school by boring through rumors that you "come from money."

6. Work two part-time jobs because your mother refuses to buy you more than two pair of shoes per year.

7. Refuse to talk to the white therapist your mother sends you to; strenuously complain to the black therapist she later finds

for you. Say things like, "I hate my mother" & "If she didn't want a black child, she shouldn't have adopted a black child." Glower a lot.

8. Get to college.

9. In a Black History class, have an Egyptian woman, preferably named Sherene, resolutely point to you & scowl, *That sister doesn't even know why she shouldn't wear the flag on her chest!*

10. At nineteen move from Chocolate City #1 where you are not really chocolate (because surely chocolate is as chocolate does) to Chocolate City #2, where you might more easily (read: without interference from your mother or her tribe) become chocolate by enrolling in a *chocolate* college, concerned with strictly chocolate issues.

11. Put to the side all paradoxical information you've learned about white people.

12. Start calling black people, "black folks," & remember to include the self in characterizations about black people such as, "Well, you know how we do," etc. . . .

13. Shake it loose, baby, double head, double tongue.

14. In Chocolate City #2 set about finding the blackest behaving people you can (define black behavior as (A) a thing,

(B) as limitedly as possible, & (C) by using TV definitions ala "Good Times" or "Sanford & Son" when possible).

15. Use the paradoxical information you've learned about white people to explain to black folks how one might point out inconsistencies between Self-Empowerment doctrines they espouse & dressing "Gucci-down." Or become a translationist.

16. Show gratitude to the black folks who accept you in spite of your "white ways" & say nice things about your mother like, "You shouldn't do her like you do," or "She's really sweet," or "She's cool," even if you don't agree.

17. Find your way to Miss Leona's house in Beltsville, Maryland & beg of her the secret of neck bones.

18. Grow to resent Miss Kevera for making you perform Jemima-style at such a young age by taking care of some pitiful, funky white boy.

19. Find, via another friend, that many black folks don't like white people. Learn this by asking, "You don't like white people, do you?" to which she'll respond, "No, I don't like Caucasoids." Hide your flinch.

20. As with #11, put to the side the paradoxical information you've learned about black folks.

21. Move to New York City where racial designations are tricky. Fall in with a crowd. Learn what being Jewish means.

49

Realize Heather from 4th grade was Jewish. Wonder how difficult life must have been for Judy Kim in such a racially resolute city (Chocolate City #1). Learn what Nuyorican means. Realize Nuyorican men, with their beautiful African & European bones, are going to be a problem & wonder if this is significant in some way—or at least ironic. Begin to wonder about Cuba. Take a trip to China where poverty looks like the same bastard you saw in Morocco years before.

22. Realize that race & class are as bound as Detroit & its cars.

23. Make up to your mother.

24. Shake it loose, baby, double head, double tongue.

25. Go to a poetry reading where you hear Sonia Sanchez calling everyone *brother* & *sister* & believe her.

26. Get tired of the double head, double tongue & while in grad school, lay plum pulp & honey to your hands callused from the weight of your heads & tongues. Get a job. Move west.

27. Watch your mother die.

28. Stop for a moment. Stop.

29. Begin anew.

30. Realize it is in the nature of most animals to gorge themselves until they are satiated.

31. When a friend who adopts a child of difference asks how your mother raised such a balanced black woman, look out into the great wing of the sky & say *Love*, & say *Patience*.

32. Wonder what happened to Marshall & if he needs plums & honey.

33. &, as is the way with so many tribes over these many, many years, as is the way of so many women, like your mother, lay your hands open, give over your particular body to the world, leave your wounds to writhe, dip your toes in the past to check its temperature, but not before you ask for forgiveness. & not before you raise your head & say, *Amen*.

Race

What kind of love is this we have
that our words walk between us,
an odd couple,
married & cobbling along
the streets of a city.
They are ermine & cashmere,
dusty & leaning into each other,
the eyes of one stopping
where the second eyes begin.

So what if we are old?
We are not too ridden with time.
Undress your words, my Love,
let them hang loose as my breasts.
Let them suckle or spit, but here
where once they took pleasure.
Let it be said, this silence. Let it be loosed.
Let the corset & cummerbund,
the cold, shimmering stockings spill down.

The Swifts
Portland, OR

We folks blanket & body the hill
while the swifts churn above the chimney,
forty thousand strong. We watch wondering
at their many bodies. & suddenly one goes down.
They all go down. A black bullet
into that impossible space.

Two days ago my neighbor's son
stabbed a black man. Later on the same night
he & a friend leveled a gun at another man,
black again, like me.

The news reports them as skinheads.
Supposedly, he was their most violent.
But he is a boy, square in the shoulder,
flat stomached. Sometimes a blank look
takes his face when he doesn't understand.
He often doesn't understand.

What I know of him says he is no skinhead.
But I know less as my days grow longer.
The proof is that he is in jail, probably huddling
with his Aryan brothers. I will never forget the sound
of my name in his mouth. It was friendly there.
& helpful. Offering—& bloodless.

It's only now that fear takes hold of my body,
remembering how close our bodies had been,
some two doors away,
close like the bodies of my students
who tonight are full of innocence & awe,
who cluster on this blanket
watching the birds dart into their hole
& sleep deep into their lives.
What travesties will befall them?
I think I once had an answer to these questions,
when I was young & full of spit & able to seethe.
But I do not know what it was, where it has gone,
the answer. What will my students become?
How will their bodies color & shape the world?
How will they duck & dart & will I have to?
No matter how I try I don't want them here on my blanket,
at all, ever.

This

~ *after Adrienne Rich*

I tell you,

  this sack,

    this sock, thew & vein,

has been

  a chronic

    problem, a condition,

an other

  around which

    I work. I am a super duper

navigator,

  have been

    jacques cousteauing

for years,

  & I'm telling you, this

    has been a chronic problem:

this body

  against which

    the world, upon which

the world,

  & the me of it

    inside as if a bean or a bead,

a kernel

  of something, maybe

    a glimmer, a chunk of ore,

hard & steadfast
      & improbably mashed.
            I tell you, this is a problem
of too little
      language, a lie—this body,
            conundrum, this other me, me
this body, this,
      this, I tell you, this
            is not me, I tell you. Not me.

Race Card

Dear Mr. Burke,

As you might remember from our conversation, my mom gave me this Race Card (enclosed as per your request) at the beginning of the year because my college said that every freshman needed one. But I never used mine. My aunt had already bought my textbooks & everything else in the campus store seemed sort of goofy & irrelevant. So since I haven't used it & probably won't ever, I contacted your department hoping to either get a refund or an exchange.

I really appreciate the huge exception you're making for me (&, as per your request, I have not mentioned this to any of my classmates, although, most have used their Race Cards anyway). I realize you can't give me refund but *can* exchange the Race Card for some other type of gift card. After thinking about it for a while, I think a grocery store gift card would be best. $50 will buy lots of Ramen noodles!

Anyway, I know you said your daughter is my age & is in college in Maryland. I hope she's enjoying it there as much as I am here & that someone in Maryland is as kind to her as you've been to me. Thanks again.

Sincerely,

Anza Jenesis Jones
Class of 2012

Parable of Kings & Queens

~ after Jack

Up & down MLK Blvd. the story jabbers about,
pops upside LaShawn's head. LaShawn
who is cutting school & her eyes,
waps along the sidewalks
where Marcus gets his mack on,
where Tika is dragging her son who wants
a lollipop, wants a lollipop, wants, wants
a lollipop.

According to some, before the white folks came & got us,
it was all good. Africa was a land of plenitude & glory
where no one went poor or hungry, no one slapped his wife
as if she were a fly, no wife smacked her child.

The days shimmered long
& only just hot enough to be comfortable,
nights were full of lovemaking
wherein hands were held, souls were made one,
& regal children were produced.

In Africa we were better. We were not ourselves.

Not one of us cut our eyes or sucked our teeth
or was trifling or stinky or dumb. Not one of us
was a jive ass fool just sorta walkin' around.

Sugar, or
Parable on Liberals

Girl, when his tongue is all sugar, suddenly
sweetened on the way u walk & dress,
be careful. When he begins to see u as candy,
something to be sucked on & swallowed,
look to his feet. Is he walkin' ure way
or are his dogs tucked beneath him?
That carpet is all magic & mirrors,
Babydoll. In the beginning was the word
but then there was feet: be wary of
the pigeon-toed fool barely steppin'
& offerin' too much sugar for a nickel.

Give Way

It would take four days
for the bird to give way.
& in each of the days I stood inside
watching the bucket on the balcony,
wondering what bit of curiosity
had drawn the swallow down
to the blue mopping bucket
against which his muting body
desperately crashed. On the fourth day
I stepped outside, but only after
the bird's thrashing had quieted
to a despondent thump.
    I had seen a body dying
before, had known then too
what was happening, understood, although
I did not have the language for it
that the thing in us that is light & breezy
& that we love
thrashes & then dwindles,
sometimes coughing, sometimes moaning,
sometimes simply sitting quietly
& offering his body's warm wrinkled knee.
I was too young then to do anything
but watch my father die
& when I was not near him,
imagine my father dying.
    I too am constantly giving way:
Yesterday in the store & the man,

the day before on the sidewalk & the woman,
each diminishment a subtle transaction.
Today, this is the way you will pay. & you must
pay you black, you woman, your shiny token
or find another bleak means of egress.
       So no, that small bird, poor pitiful thing,
whose life I might have spared
by turning the bucket to its side,
garnered nothing free or merciful from me
or my understanding.
What more I can repeat is music of the dark,
dark seed in my eye whispering back
this insidious something I had learned, learn,
resist over & over: swallow, swallow, yield!

Cut

Somewhere in the world is a book written by a woman about a woman, her arms extending into the muck & slime of reddened dishwater. She's in her new place, where the phone hangs limply on the wall & people smile limply & her tongue lies limply in her mouth before it curls & spits, lashes out beside itself. It's another Friday night & she peers through the window at the big tree, thinks to find its name one day, considers how the sun beds itself so contentedly, how it shines regardless of locus, sees it anew, again. & the stone path there, the stones on the path are as years laid out in a crooked & gnarled taunt. & though she cannot see their beginning she certainly sees them leading languidly to the base of an ugly, nameless tree. She thinks of her hand, her blood & that, all things considered, there should be a man propped against that bark, grinning or waving his crazy arms. Or, at least a friend who would call, not back, just call. & she cannot, no matter how many times she stands in this place, watching the sun's slide, wondering at the name of that tree, she cannot pattern a way to escape the dishes. We all eat, she says to herself. We all reach down knowing the water will sting.

God Is Good
birthday poem

Someone is always saying: This year is a good year,
this twenty-fifth year, this thirty-first year.
Someone is always pointing, however coyly, to God.
More of this, more of that, they chirp, it's all good:
Understanding will blossom like a girl's breasts—slowly
until they are, it is, a fact.

Today my accomplishments crouch in the corner,
not jabbering happily or raising their hands,
but with their grubby heads down murmuring something dull.

I have never heard the clock's boom or listened
to the ground's gossip, to the trees' riddles, never wanted
to be a woman running naked through the woods—
there were so many more reasonable things to do.
Yet this morning a moan, again the dusty candle, again an eye
to the makeshift temple in the room I never fully inhabit.

Today *is* dark & I *am* on the ground, the trees *do* sigh,
the clock *does* beat. & what to do with this noise?
Maybe this is the good life, this sudden uncertainty.
Maybe this is the woman all women once were.
Maybe this is the way: the body as quiver—a chronic, quaking
receptacle to be simply asserted, inserted,
pressed again & again between the God & the Good.

At Lincoln's Feet

Today on the steps of the Lincoln Memorial,
surrounded by the wavering facets of our world,
a remembrance of my mother's story: me
crawling up the chest of drawers,
its great bulk heaving forward,
the pain, panic, long shriek of it.
These memories are not mine, are gone,
gone even among these shards is my four year old body,
the quizzical rationale, all but some faint knowledge
to do with weight & how a body so easily pins beneath it.

Today on the steps of the Lincoln Memorial,
surrounded by the old facets of our world,
the stuff of our inheritance reflects brilliantly
in the basin pool. Here, here are whispers & flickers,
ghosts fussing, wanting to tell their side of it.

That we inherit more than eye color or temperament
is an old, reliable story. But if the memories that matter
lose their intimate details, are more nebulous & necessary
than histories of the brief, habitual eruptions we are born to
& from which we cannot escape?

& if we are emanations, each, & even as we give way
are simply fragments & to-be figments,
some form of ancient & enchanted memory?
What if the thousands of bodies on that dreamy day,
pressing deeply against & into each other

64

of a single beat & will
manifested as low level emissions,
etching against the great blue board of the sky?
& if we learned to read before we learned to read?

Wouldn't it be wisest for us to trust
our quickenings, to retrain, act, react
not in light of language, but in honor of
a wan, warm thump, here.

Jubilee

The next day I had already nearly forgotten
a cat once lived here, packed up her bowl
& personals, went about my business.
Now, the psychic claims she is still in my room,
padding on the bed, queen of the realm, waiting,
willing to relinquish space for the right man.
The psychic has been wrong for years.
There is no man who will make life better.
& anyway, I remember one of the last nights
Jubilee cozied up: the vague unmoving lump on my foot,
the dark kick, the cat fly. Not a good omen.

I wonder if that beautiful black girl would recount our
slow moan, how we grew apart, each silent,
circling & nodding, the times she insisted on my lap
& I resisted. Or would she demur, be gracious & recall
visitors: my mother's gentle hands,
friends & their soft warm laps? Would she mewl:
Well, yes. Behind closed doors
the heart ceases its public prance. But.
Love is love.

Old Town

Portland, OR

Leopold is teething. Like all dogs who are sweet
but not too bright, our *no's!* haven't worked.

Two guys approach wanting to cop
a quick pet because Leopold is damned cute.

They ask permission of Robert who answers
I'd prefer it if you don't. He's in training. This is a lie

& code, really, for *God no, you're too skanky.*
In Old Town, the half million dollar

renovated warehouse town homes haven't yet come.
Someone drew the line in the sand six blocks up, two over,

pulled the fanciness to an abrupt halt.
We live amid the remnants of a certain ghetto.

Things are getting better, improvement noses
about, searches out more territory. At Burger King

you can no longer engage in loud conversations
& must eat & leave within twenty minutes.

The list of rules is long as the meth clinic line
which is as long as the soup kitchen line;

all in these four small blocks
& filled with the same sad men.

& even though I've just moved from New York,
where sad men seem sadder, my morning jaunts are telling:

cross the street when one approaches, avoid Broadway
& Burnside, don't speak. This is what I've become.

I've always hastened to treat everyone equally.
That I hasten tells on me. I recognized Robert's code

too quickly & was thankful. Only now,
after a day has passed, do I consider that the men asked

to pet the dog. I never do, just assume, bend down,
expect a wag, an acknowledgment

that I might have been the one to love him,
a welcome with full body contact,

without words or their exemptions.

The same sort Leopold would have given
those sad-eyed men who perhaps only wanted
to remember.

Patience [aloud]

Patience was raised by his momma, Faith—a round woman with breasts that settled well onto her stomach. If your eyes could get up past these, you'd see she had a beautiful face, angelic really. As a child, Pat never noticed the particularity of these mounds except to say his mother was soft, the softest person in the world. Of course, he didn't mean like a feather bed or a cloud or even a mass of cotton candy. He meant that when he cried she was softly around him, smoothing all the roughness, whispering to him, making everything seem possible & hopefully small. Once when he was eight, he swore he saw wings poking out of her bathrobe, but never mentioned this to anyone. As an adult Pat had grown more & more like Faith, round & big, a marshmallow, his daughter said; something, she said, you always wanted—no matter how full up with other stuff you were. But there was darkness. When the world whirred its strange, dull hum, he went into his den, shunned the sun, lamented & remembered his mother. His mother making fruit cakes for neighbors, kindly & mean. When he asked why she baked for Hildregard Deceit who even now was stooped over with his own venom, hobbling down the street, poking his stick well in front of him, scowling, cursing the children & sputtering indefinitely about change, comeuppance, & some unrecognizable god, Faith would gaze through the kitchen crystals & say, *The act, Patience, is itself redemptive. We must practice, Love. Pay no attention to the recipient.*

Marathon: Ars Poetica

From fifteen stories up
          I cannot make out their faces
but can see the outline
          of their sharpened bodies,
men first, then a smattering
          of women, then the horde,
both types of bodies
          in effulgent color;
arms, feet, heartbeats in rhythm
          & forcing forward.

There is no real reason
          I should grow weepy.
They are just myriad bodies,
          willful human stories
moving against the brisk Chicago wind.
          There is no reason at all
to be so moved except
          the other faithful people
lining the streets in such early morning
          chanting & rahing
& banging their tambourines.

Glutton

~ after Miki, the Scottish Terrier

Birds feather their own nests, & so yes, you are reminded it is in our nature to be self-fulfilling. You bend to her because the universe demands it: what is asked is needed. Let us say on days when you walk into the office she is often on her dark back in aisle's middle, furry appendages stretched obscenely skyward, bare belly soft & sloping & open to wounding. She is undeniable, a pull: rub, here, now, like this. There is something about trust, here, some lesson to do with openness & submission, the stubborn nature converted. There is something exquisite about asking for love so nakedly, so patiently, everyday, Miki: a teacher, every office day, walking through the world a vessel, a glutton. Let us mute. Let us bend or stretch but say, yes—this is the way we can hope it to be. This world, this rub. Yes, let us say.

About the Author

Born in 1970, Crystal Williams was raised in Detroit, Michigan and Madrid, Spain. She attended Wayne State and Howard universities where she studied acting before dropping out of school to more seriously pursue a theatre career in New York City. There Williams began her formal involvement with poetry at the Nuyorican Poets Café, finding in Slam a complimentary synthesis between writing and performance. She is a member of the 1995 Nuyorican Slam Team. She went on to earn a Bachelor of Arts degree at New York University and a Master of Fine Arts at Cornell University. She is currently Associate Professor at Reed College in Portland, Oregon and divides her time between Portland and Chicago, Illinois.